Giacomo Ponti

Dato Magradze

trans Natalia Bukia-Peters & Victoria Field

fal

First published in Georgian in Tbilisi in 2011

This translation published by

fal publications
9, The Crescent
Canterbury
CT2 7AQ
UK

Translation copyright, 2012

Natalia Bukia-Peters
Victoria Field

Cover design, Levan Titmeria and Dato Magradze

A CIP record for this book is available from the British Library

ISBN 978-0-9555661-3-4

Printed in Cornwall by R.Booth Ltd

Foreword

This is how the man speaks,

this is how he expresses his concerns, he speaks in this way

to nourish his soul, to create a cornucopia of good things.

To put it simply, this is just the way he happens to speak.

He's not doing it to impress anyone or become famous.

When he speaks in this pleasing way,

it's like escaping the unbearable heat of summer to the cool seaside.

And it's like listening to a story or fable,

one that's familiar, or one that's from faraway.

One person scolded the man, another praised him.

What does he want, why does he behave like a victim?

He's expressing his sadness, this is he how he speaks.

Who is he?

I think he's a poet.

This is how the man speaks.

Prologue to the poem, Giacomo Ponti

An alarm clock's rattle shooting through the morning,
individual sachets of coffee offered up in offices,
and Pontius Pilate, the plumber who controls the household taps,
all bring the exile of this man closer.

Questions about time have become my enemy.
Does time march in front of me
or am I ahead of time?
Now, my best suit's covered in dust,
but, who cares, nothing special will happen for me to wear that suit.

The fresco of the saint has faded
just like my childhood's disappeared in the mirror,
all I see
is what remains of what once was me.
It's as if the garden has walked away from the gardener.

Everywhere I go, I encounter such sad eyes
and before a shaft of sunlight will break through to touch this paper
the words I'm sending you
teeter like clowns on a tightrope.

This Oriental-Western divan
will be replaced by shelves laden with books
when the poet can make a necklace of water droplets
from a spring bursting through leaf-covered rocks,

when he's done up his unbuttoned collar
and his stories of kisses have become tired gossip,
when the publishers carry his words ashore
and lay them down in a sunny spot on the kind bank

and a fresco showing your profile remains in
the story about a man who slid down the ridge of the mountain,
showing something from the past,
something
which has yet to appear in print,

when the poet's courage is threaded through the adverts
on the posters, battered by wet wind in the open air-café
on the old square, or scattered among pigeons
who strut about among truth and falsehoods.

A kind of glue dropped between the words
also brings back precisely old shots of an earlier life,
your grandmother leaning over the cast iron balcony
waiting for you as day breaks.

She blesses you with the sign of the cross when you leave
sends a guardian angel to take care of you.
What sort of women were they, sitting around drinking tea,
discussing whether a white collar was really white?

I flounder in the darkness of thoughts and memories,
like the bow of my violin, trying to make contact with the strings.
Like a young man standing on the night shore, I gaze,
watching my ship sink over the horizon.

I'm the youth from whom fate took away luck,
from whom the February sun stole the snow.
I'm the one who didn't turn up for the general rehearsal,
and failed to get the leading role.

In a wet dawn, he leaned against drenched lines of poetry
using them as crutches, the way, during a drought,
vines slump against their stakes
waiting for the rain to give its verdict.

In a wet dawn, he leaned against drenched lines of poetry,
carrying the tang of salt from night waves.
They have courage, declare
'What will be, will be!' to Christ the Lord.

In a wet dawn ... I said it again,
not just twice, but a third time,
because I was saying goodbye to people,
like an officer says goodbye to his stripes.
Such farewells broke my heart.

The tavern suffices to shelter me,

there's the warmth of a felt hanging behind me,

as I sing a song of someone besieged.

I'll force my smoke rings into crowns of thorns.

My love, all these Amazonian women in the tavern

will create a muddle, fanning themselves forever,

in vino, vino,

vino veritas …

I say it over and over again, craning my neck.

The immoral elite doesn't know how to behave …

I sit, trying to clear my mind of unpleasant thoughts,

those of the sharp oath and samurai sword

can't bear the wiggle of a bottom.

I lived in this town as a callow youth,

destiny did not, and could not, turn me into an idiot

and now I'm singing, in a new register,

bare-chested, my collar unbuttoned – RRRRidi Pagliaccio …

Today's newspaper informs me

the state, this very one,

will use its legal processes to bury

the great leaps forward made by inspiration

and an individual citizen turned into the masses.

He will bring into himself

the events of outside.

He'll choose something from the bookshelf,
it'll probably be the book for registering complaints.

And we, well, we'll carry on as usual,
digging our own trenches drenched in stinky vodka,
what else can we do? Huh?
We'll get together a bevy of beautiful wenches.

But sometimes the world is so illuminated,
I want to put my head under the cold water tap,
refusing to allow Pilate to approach the water
and let you hear the songbirds, barking like dogs.

Chapter I   This Earthly Life

From the house of the father ...

To the house of the Father ...

Chapter II Courtroom

The lights are on in the courtroom,
where life is priced according to the waiting,
the lawyer by the door takes a last draw on his cigarette.
All stand,
it's time for justice!

The following case will be heard:
Giacomo Ponti stands accused,
along with the precipices
and pinnacles of his soul,
this captain of a fleet of paper boats:

I, citizen Giacomo Ponti,
descended from the families of Cosimo and Lorenzo
have always fought on the front line,
while living in fear of life passing me by.

Look at the light emanating from this sacred book,
I put my hand on what is sacred, and on justice,
swearing I will tell the whole truth,
and nothing but the truth.

I don't really remember how I got here,
I was drunk, and it seemed as if I sat on a stem of cress.
Perhaps the stem of cress gave way,
I fell off and now stand accused.

I citizen Giacomo Ponti,
of Cosimo and Lorenzo's line
... I really don't remember
how I got here,
I certainly don't mean to make a fuss in public.

I swear on the names of my ancestors,
and of knights loyal to their king,
that I defended with my blood the land of the Grail,
but what's that got to do with anything?

I, citizen Giacomo Ponti,
hereby declare, however you put the charges,
whatever you're accusing me of is completely pointless,
there's no way I will plead guilty.

I made myself familiar with this groundless case,
with every detail of their accusations,
saw the lawyer wiggling his hips on the spot,
competently as a belly dancer.

I want to defend myself,
become my own counsel for the defence,
to return to you, for better or worse
any accusation you've pitifully invented.

Please, pay close attention to every statement,
any expression of emotion is out of place here,
you can receive three years in prison
for contempt of court.

If I am accused of believing in a dream,
or of wishing life is just one long holiday,
or if I add some details, or withhold others,
let this whole morning go to hell.

I admit, I'm guilty of one thing,
that I accused you of love.
I am in debt, owe much more than a penny,
I took my share from crime.

I failed to build a nest on your roof top,
and I let the curtain drop during your performance,
it's a saving grace when kindness
can be seen in a crime.

Moses is taking me to the promised tavern
where the lines of my old poems,
buried in the background of your new epoch
will mellow like an old cognac.

Chapter III Letter to Achilles

Hey, Achilles!
I couldn't find any fault in her,
the lady on the high hills,
I couldn't take her clothes off, couldn't make her
succumb to Apollo's arrow.
I don't know why, perhaps when she was young
she was dipped head to toe
in a whirlpool in the River Styx
and rendered untouchable.
Which way should I go?
Advise me, Achilles my hero,
invite me to ride inside a wooden horse
to the walls of Troy, as Peter
on the waves of the sea, and perish
time after time in a battle for heroes.
Let my name sound through the centuries...
Or perhaps I should tempt fate again,
take the lady down to the shore.
She'll find walking difficult on her high heels,
maybe, maybe, I'll persuade her to come down
from her proud pedestal.
She'll be cheered up by going barefoot
and with the footprints of her inspiration
I'll make her write on the wet sand
a line of this poem.
It will be drenched in moonlight,
that moist line.

Chapter IV Courtroom

When you gave the eye
to the wife of the Mayor of Vererie,
you tempted her and possessed her.
Do you plead guilty?
No, Sir.

And now, here in this court,
you look at her broken heart and smile.
What can we attribute your excitement to?
Do you admit your guilt?
No, Sir.

You promised her, as she says herself,
only the night sky and sky diamonds...
Only this and just an innocent kiss.
Do you plead guilty?
No, Sir.

Love was sculpted into shape,
love waited for Rodin and he gave it form.
The sea and the setting sun were witnesses
as, too, were the wide shore and wet sand.

Let someone question them,
where else in the world would you find such trustworthy witnesses?
Come on, cross-examine them all,

one by one, if you like,
or if you prefer, all together.

They don't need to swear on the Bible,
nor prove their identities,
we followed the night through the moonshine
like a foal follows its mother, the mare.

Come on, discard the letter of the law.
Instead question the wave and wet sand,
if you encounter a language barrier,
I'll interpret every single sign.

I'll translate how the wave breaks,
how, with the tip of a tongue, waves lick bodies,
the first star appearing high above
touches the spume of the breaking wave.

Yes, I did give this lady the eye.
I didn't try to blind her to reality,
I gave her, according to the laws of nature
the missing other half she'll never find again.

We two caressed in the carriage of night,
we were patinas caressing a bronze,
I will say to the Eve of that night:
Your complaint against me has injured my ribs.

Even if you leave a village woman in the lurch,
she'd drink wine before complaining,
and, just like a loaf rising in a hot oven
she'd envelop you in her soft, warm bed.

You're judging a woman's fantasy
at the jagged edge of conventional morality,
where dreams do the kissing,
you'll look in vain for someone to carry the guilt.

Like one follows a flock of cranes in the sky,
I followed the lines of the poem.
You can't see me
because I don't exist,
it was the women who invented me.

I am telling you, Giacomo Ponti,
you're judging the reason for the dream,
you're trying Carmen's motive
and finding Bizet guilty.

These discussions with you are going on and on,
I don't think I can take any more,
so I'll hum Carmen's motif, if you'll allow me,
as an example.

Ta,ram,tam,tam,

Ta,ram,tam,tam,

Ta,ram ram,ra,ra,ra,ra,

Ra,ra,ro!

Ba-ram,bam,bam!

Ra,ra,ra,ro,

Ra,ra,ra,ra-ra-ri-ri-ro, riiii…

Ra,ro!

This musical confession,

is worth its weight in gold,

although it goes without saying whenever we celebrate,

there's an element of crime.

I, citizen Giacomo Ponti,

hereby declare, however you put the charges,

whatever you're accusing me of is completely pointless,

there's no way I will plead guilty.

You want the truth. I've already poured out

the poison which was given to me, I've left the front line

and I've laid to rest without ceremony,

deep in my body, the late Giacomo Ponti.

I'm now a coffin in the castle,

with the flags lowered and chandeliers extinguished.

Exile me, to the country of my own body
where I'll skim through my sentence, as if it were milk.

I am already reduced to bones
because I was given a cruel destiny.
Because I emptied every bit of poison out of me,
I'm now full of my emptiness.

Chapter V Sleeping Poem

A girl sleeps peacefully in bed,
the room was worn out by the glass of wine.
The emptied glass is standing like …
Let's just leave it without any comparison.

And a poem sleeps peacefully in this thought,
unadorned, in the country of sleep.
So I don't startle it, I'll break the rhyme,
it won't wake up without a rhyme.

The girl is asleep like a poem,
how close I feel to something that seems so far away,
I'll choose a name for this sleeping symbol,
or perhaps I'll leave it without a metaphor.

At her head, I'll place a sleeping poem,
as an invitation to this new book.
I'll leave the book's door open
and wait until she enters.

I won't do up her unbuttoned dress,
I'll trust that to her guardian angel,
I'll let the poem touch her and wake her,
she will button up the front of her dress herself.

The sleeping poem,

the sleeping woman,

her face unmade up, no lipstick.

The drunken poet who serves the morning star

is answerable for the noise of the waking day ...

He's accountable to the people,

they'd make him responsible for the resurrection,

it was he who took the woman out into the rain,

made a gift to the rain of both the woman and power.

He gave the rain to the woman,

the woman to the rain,

heedless of customs and the Sabbath,

and when he fell down drunk in the street,

the rain and the soaked dress rushed to him.

He gave life to the rain and the woman,

he roused the sleeping poem,

the old familiar cry echoed once again:

Crucify him,

this shepherd of the rain drops!

Chapter VI Aperitif before the Presentation

I had spurs on my heels
and loosened the reins,
I was riding a galloping horse, searching for
the Star of Bethlehem and holiness.

I want to make a statement to you all,
standing quite still, as the witnesses jostle around,
I buried the remains of my grandfather
in the earth of my native land, as if dropping an anchor.

Grandfather

Chapter VII   Overture to the Presentation

So be it, I'll never recapture the aura of my dream of the white deer,

my only protection will be the heaven of poetry,

unless I make equal obeisance

to the pale-faced lady from Europe,

and Khanum, the Oriental woman with a mole.

Chapter VIII To the Pale-faced Lady

Under the umbrella, the rain nudges

The Kiss as sculpted by Rodin,

with your lips sweeten her lips,

with your heel locate the hem of her dress.

The women, the umbrella and the boulevard

will know much heavier rain.

She won't refuse an old client

in the freshness of newly fallen rain.

Like an open fan, she'll cover pains born of creation

with the words au revoir.

Chapter IX To the One with a Mole

Melehat Khanum,

go on, swear on the name of your old pimp mother,

the one who turned you into a hooker,

praying for you to Allah

in the Blue Mosque,

she sniggered at heaven,

flashing it her gold teeth,

winking at Muhammad.

Chapter X Presentation on the East-West Divan

… when Zeus noticed how
beautiful Europe was,
he immediately rushed with the bullskin
to the Asia he'd created himself
and carried away the virgin on his back.

Own epigraph

They're swindlers along the old trade routes,
at the crossroads of Europe and Asia,
my country abandoned to fate by its location,
I shed tears in the shape of the motherland.

My country, veined by the old silk routes
weaves through my dreams,
an Oriental appetite
striving for the life of a Westerner.

These roads were the net of my nervous system,
teaching me the wisdom of ancient Athens,
illuminated along their lengths
by the shimmer
of Isfahan's light.

The enemy watched it all with its vigilant eye,
how an avalanche fell on the narrow roads,

sometimes I think that
culture is simply
the history of self-restraint.

How some people kill their passions at birth,
thinking it's worth curbing every desire,
a man following the will of his priest,
with sunshine and dreams,
practising patience and will-power.

Here are three Commanders from Europe,
you, Horatio,
lend me your ear,
from Athens, rationality!
from Rome, justice!
and faith belongs to Jerusalem.

Jesus gave Europe its soul,
he touched Saul, turned him into Paul,
and, as if a curtain was opened,
the East was bewitched.

The East is difficult to fathom,
its elegance has its own charisma,
waves on the Marmara stitch themselves into knots,
the salty Bosphorus gives off ozone caresses.
The East advances on the West,
I let go of my horse's reins.

If you want, you can call me
Bosphorus, I'm like the straits,
one water with two mouths.

I ignited the tinder with the steel of my poem,
moulded destiny in my own way,
inhaled air from the lungs of Christ,
and wrote with all the elegance of Islam.

So, what? Peter the Great created his window to Europe,
his fine city letting in fresh air,
here, nine centuries ago, Ferdowsi
wrote his epic, Shahnameh.

The light of Nizami shone constantly
in Giacomo Ponti's village and city,
sometimes his homeland bugled its music
through the vertebrae of Byzantium's spine.

... yet, sadly, I long for honeyed love,
I want to fill my heart with it,
with rainbows and subtle hues,
I want to be convinced by the East.

There, colours are more than colours,
colours embrace the whole universe,
words are too small to contain them,
they offer up a face and a soul on a tray.

When colours speak instead of words,
an apprentice doing his master's bidding
can manifest Khosrow and Shirin's mighty empire,
telling its story in miniatures.

I'm going off the point now,
but the reader may be interested to know,
if I whisper just one story.
Do you want my name?
I'm red.

My rival's name is yellow,
he killed our blue master,
seized the buyer of souls,
dipping his brush into red.

When in the king's garden, fruits are ripe,
the king makes his own myths,
anyone who doesn't blush red with shame,
will find himself red with blood stains.

This is a story from far away,
told at the fence around the Sultan's tower
and when the autumn came,
dry leaves blushed red then yellow.
This is a story from far away,
a far-away story told in whispers.
One artist remained out of two,
the story was never printed.

As for what concerns Christian Europe,
it sometimes runs away like water through fingers,
Europe dedicates the church of Delle Grazie to supper,
and sometimes lucratively searches for the Da Vinci code.

Lilies on the banners of Santa Maria,
are teased by a late wind,
a Viennese orchestra floats as if at sea
and von Karajan lifts his baton like Moses.

The chandelier's switched off, its crystal still ringing,
I'm sitting, ruminating in an all-night café.
Emptiness in fine clothes
is the poster of our epoch.

It's no good only dancing for tourists,
Spanish passion needs more sun,
poplar trees have grown over bones buried over bones,
Europe's become an exhibit in a museum case.

But this man is such an expert judge of colour,
there's no doubt about his ability to argue his case.
He can match a tatty coat
perfectly to his shirt.
He remembers Michelangelo.

If you remove the worn-out exhibits
and revive their old glory,
tell them what they no longer know,
blow the soul into those inanimate objects,

after seven days, you must strive for an eighth,
in order for the flamenco sun to get hotter,
from the stretched nerves, like strings of an instrument,
you have to talk to them
and let them talk.

And to paint the old door in a new way,
the old and deep universe waits,
as Lazarus waited to be touched,
a new life,
with his old expression.

Doubts still torture you,
the ringing of bells frightens you,
now and then, its past or current beauty.
It is or is not,
is or is not.

Is not, is,
is not, is,
but the Pieta, the mountains of Carrara ...

Maybe it's over, or perhaps it's still going on,
the current celebration of Mass, or the one that's just past...

Hope's once again hindered by doubt,
they've announced a great sale of souls,
our epoch lies fallen, gnawed at by doubts,
surrounded by wounded thoughts.

Flesh has been sacrificed to the soul,
just as you sacrificed your family to the poem,
rain falls on bare breasts,
as a sword reaches the loyal Mujahid.

I blame no one for what's happened to me,
I bathed in the steamy waters of the Trevi Fountain,
I defended the Grail like a crusader,
I wandered like a dervish.

The horse's reins are loosened,
the East advances on the West...
I am the two mouths of one water,
if you want, call me Bosphorus.

Chapter XI The Old Church of the Village

The church is clearly visible, but no great excitement.

Green mould velvets the walls.

What modest splendour,

what splendid modesty.

Chapter XII TV Broadcast

A tsunami hit Japan,

no one knows how many died.

Gucci launched a new perfume.

Ashes around Vesuvius await tourists.

Patriots from Georgia

continue their laborious research into

the constituents of Tolstoy's blood,

just how much of it is Russian?

Libya's opened a new front line,

Chanel's opened a cat rescue centre,

Giacomo Ponti is on trial,

the prosecution is his own people.

Chapter XIII My Compatriot's E-mail

patriot-pateticum@yahoo.com

Chapter XIV My Other Compatriot's E-mail

gayliberta-progress@yahoo.com

Chapter XV Summary of the Two Previous Chapters

The first one wasn't patriotic
and the second one wasn't liberal.
Both were children
of a cursed Georgia.

Chapter XVI In Modern Georgian

They attend confession in the morning, receive absolution,

in order to greet their mother and father,

then, with money won at the casino,

buy drugs for their neighbours.

I'm an historian chronicling the contemporary,

I see an epoch that won't last long.

We're told by 'brain-storming'

'fund-raising' is achievable.

A girl who falls in love at the drop of a hat, talks

with the froth of liberalism around her mouth.

Come on, I'm leaving

but I'll be back like Theseus,

carrying my sword and a ball of thread.

Chapter XVII Reform

Just as the photo of Monica Bellucci in the toilet

protects the rights of the right hand,

in the same way, the tricksy authorities

come prematurely,

torturing the old pricks.

Chapter XVIII Phone Call to Friends. Globalisation

I seem to be surrounded by goats.

You came to mind, you have seen so much.

Someone asks me about friendship,

what's happened to that word?

Chapter XIX Meeting with the Motherland

My country, whatever you are, if
you ceased to exist, I'd never be able to replace you,
I love whatever you have the potential to be,
I love what you can never be.
                    Own epigraph

When we meet, snow will start falling,
there'll be wind and rain, tears precious as diamonds,
my motherland will come to this rendezvous,
touch you with her lips, then betray you.

The motherland will come to pollinate your soul,
to teach you the laws, to bring executioners.
The motherland will come like a sacrificial altar,
hold you in her embrace, then betray you.

The motherland comes with open arms,
and doesn't need sweet talking,
she'll brand you on your forehead,
in order to decorate you with ribbons,
in order to sacrifice you like a lamb.

If you could turn into dust and ashes,
after turning, finding the light for sunset,
or if you suffer for your own motherland
like you suffer for your own adventures,

if you attempt to summon morning
by crying out at dawn like a cockerel,
the motherland will sneak up slyly, jinxing you,
even the unlucky black cat will sell you out.

It's hard to find your motherland from inside,
she rushes on, whizzing past you,
fast as a car on the unmade roads,
leaving your eyes tearful from the flying dust.

If you enter the sacred palisade,
shining rays will reach you.
It's hard to find your motherland from inside,
she's trying to make you worthy of a memorial.

The motherland is intuitive and capable,
she tests your strength under a higher authority.
If you act like you can't care less,
she'll erect a monument after your death.

You'll be lost under rain and snow,
she wants that false patriot with his furrowed brow,
if a man should appear in the courtyard of the church,
that false patriot will drag him in by his beard.

Your motherland will send a band of robbers after you,
on a dark road at night. That's how she expresses love for her child,

readying Golgotha for you, or
the Tsitsamuri forest where guns are often fired.

This fervent surrogate of a man thinks
he can create a prince out of the mud of himself,
his aggressive illiteracy
is mistaken in our country for patriotism.

Traditional vodka with beef and garlic soup,
the sacred revenge of a patriot's saint,
coarse wool protecting his head from the vicious sun,
retribution, and his pungent socks.

This is a new version of an old ignorance,
and the old ways are themselves a target,
a clerk's grimacing and aggression
is what we now label liberalism.

No, a motherland isn't the same as God,
it's looking for a niche close to God,
after rain and after wind
it shows, nevertheless, some sign of God.

Chapter XX Address from the Courtroom

Hey, people of Tbilisi, like people of Athens,
throw me a glance like sparks from a fire,
so that I stay close to base
and defend myself like Socrates.

The trap was laid this morning,
as the mirror watched me doing up my tie.
I'll remember what your face represents,
I'll deal with the strict bones of the law.

Rustle up your slander and jealousy,
make your sullen forehead tired with thought,
turn your listening ear directly to me,
and denounce me, you hypocrites.

I'm standing in the middle of a storm
watching an angel being beaten.
It's our duty to fight the wind,
as it shakes the souls of the paparazzi.

If a prison cell is dark,
the sun will be oppressed by voices of lawlessness,
old texts will be rewritten,
words in the beginning coming at the end
and at the end, the first ones.

Now, deal the cards of your laws,

until we set out on the road to ruin.

My laws are groups of words,

I arrange them in phrases and sentences,

logical like the centuries.

Chapter XXI At the Crossroads

My fortune, what shall I say about my faith?
When, even if the black cat gives way to me,
I cross myself. Perhaps it's enough.
I'd like to rhyme a different life for myself.

In order to say it, how to say it?
What will I say
to celebrate the glory of my native land?
But if it's in the spirit of greedy Luarsab Tatkaridze,
no one will care less.

Chapter XXII Letter to Prometheus

Hey, Prometheus!

Can you give me a light?

Pass me your Ronson,

let's puff away together, let's empty our thoughts.

Like you I wasn't allowed

to play with fire in my childhood.

But secretly I stole a box of matches,

bought cheap cigarettes

and inhaled deeply in the doorways

with guys from my district.

I gave out tongues of fire from matches

and was often punished,

like you.

Now I'm often cold, frozen out

by the human race.

I find a match,

warm myself on its tiny flame.

I too was chained

by their indifference.

They watch me,

sometimes calling the fire brigade to extinguish

my incandescence

so the house of their dark intentions won't be seen,

so fire won't spread and can't ignite

a woman and a line of poetry,

so that a pale-faced woman doesn't leave the house
for her lover,
so she won't sit down near a fire made of burning words,
feeling sleepy on a moonlight night,
fed up with paying bills for light,
so her sincere tears don't shine
in the light of the bonfire.

One day, they'll send the fire brigade.
I'll set fire to myself
and instead of me, they'll find a heap of ashes.
It'll be a good death,
a moment of glory and a sign
of salvation.

Hey, Prometheus,
pass me your Ronson,
my great ancestor,
father and brother,
let's smoke together and empty our thoughts.

Chapter XXIII Patriotism

Thought is tempered by the shaking of souls,
my experience prompts me to say that
revenge beats like a heart in the body of patriotism,
one lot of people fighting another.

Chapter XXIV Samaia Gardens

You wait, wait, wait.
Wait, you are waiting,
At home you wait, wait, wait, you wait at home, wait.
Stones lie around unthrown,
a fear which you can't frighten away prowls around.

Father's far away. You wait, you wait,
moths chewing through his Russian greatcoat,
no one throwing stones,
those shocking, shameful stones.

The priest's stole touched the back of the head,
you recalling the father. You wait, you wait.
He's returning late after carousing at a restaurant,
with a rose and a gift of Coco Chanel in his hand,

trying to trick my mother into smiling,
regaining honourable respectability,
my mother's agitation, her fear and sadness
will be wafted away like air from a stale room.

Father abandoned us long ago,
our stronghold had no protection,
yet my childhood stays in my thoughts,
as a shield and shelter.

A small child, I sit in my father's lap,
his shoulders protecting me like mountains,
mother preparing my cough mixture,
my arm raised in refusal.

I have to inhale according to the hour glass,
my father's breath warms the back of my neck
and my fear of an alien world disappears,
as every second passes, fear lessens.

I'm consoled by my father's protection of our space,
and by the shining eyes of my mother,
my heart has slowed and pulses peacefully,
although distressed and wounded.

Here's my mother with eyes like mirrors,
over there is a mist with doubts of fear,
two worlds,
a bad one and a good one,
partitioned by father's shoulders.

Father abandoned us long ago,
and since shoulders got stuck in plywood,
my childhood stretches its hand to me,
with the ringing of bells in the sanctuary.

You wait ,wait, wait, you wait,

you wait, wait, wait at home,

stones lie around unthrown,

fearsome and frightening.

You wait, wait, wait,

lama sabachthani.

Chapter XXV Prostration

And when the mother entrusts her dear Son

to the thunderous sky, she pleads ...

Let it be equal to the Father's spirit.

Let His will be done.

Chapter XXVI Feast

The promise of the people who are clergy,
the clergy's meal of bread,
the sharp blade of the knife of the law
the promise of the Promised Land.
Here are Giacomo's heroic deeds,
and straightforwardness without any conditions.

Own epigraph

My friends visited me early today,
Zaza Shatira, Kipo and Padre.
They know the taste of Kakhetian wine,
pastures, large vineyards, upper and lower.

What is it about Kakthetian wine?
When the sun sets in the ripe clusters,
rain will come to take revenge over drought
pleasing the peasants working on their knees.

Why so much endless talk,
let's lay the table and put out the jug of wine.
We started well as usual,
only later we needed wages for wine on the table.

Everyone asked one toast of me,
and I touched on such subtle topics as the sly devil,
when there'll be the second coming of Christ,
belief in Him will be everywhere and nowhere.

The cross and crucifixion will await him on the belly
like a splash of peasant food on the priest's robe,
the control of menopausal feelings in the car,
and a number plate reading MONK 001 on the back.

The lineage of Cain at the corpse of Abel,
with his spade hidden behind his head,
Jesus will come with an open leash,
He will come as a ferocious lamb.

We'll wait for him with nests torn apart,
with nets ripped to shreds, paralysed fishermen,
with the treasury thieves turned into frescoes
like donors to the church building on the cathedral wall.

We'll wait for him in the towns and villages
with the flocks of lambs and packs of wolves,
in five star monastery complexes,
their garages full of Ferraris.

If drops of water don't reach
the out-stretched hands,
before dawn,
Pilate will go round on call
fixing the taps.

In order not to mention too often

the name of mighty God in vain, with sin and treachery,

I am writing to you, Father, a letter in reply,

I called my letter White Robe.

Chapter XXVII – White Robe

He is going to be crucified dressed only in a robe.
Crucify him!
The crowd bleats cantankerously
and, thrown like a boomerang,
the crown of thorns is coming back to us.

The people are mixed-up like the weather is,
some of them fair-minded, many of them treacherous,
the sun is setting like a garnet pinned on a cloak.
He's going to be crucified dressed only in a robe.

Thick bullet-proof windows
keep the briefcase safe,
we go to the crucifixion either in our Lexus,
or by private plane.

Risky financial deals
give rise to fears of bankruptcy,
we go … we come … we sing when we go to the crucifixion,
with our bank accounts.

The Resurrection is coming to Jerusalem,
I hear the conversation of a delegation:
We apologise for the weight of our luggage,
we're taking golden crosses to the crucifixion.

He's going to the crucifixion in a white robe.

Chapter XXVIII Courtroom

You are hearing the case of a duel,
don't expect to shed tears,
there where the dress frivolously rustles,
the duel is ambushed.

My rival was used to feuding with me in the past too,
sending venom to the laity and clergy,
I could not explain, although I curbed my anger,
I learnt then that he wrote poetry.

It seems he started telephoning my girlfriend,
my heart was immediately suspicious,
he asked her to dance at a party,
he sent her beautiful flowers.

It wasn't even 6 o'clock
when our story began,
he did not forgive me for his verse,
hushed up and unpublished.

We headed to a moonlit passage,
the tips of our knives opening the darkness,
I felt the power of a giant in my knees,
fulfilled what I had promised.

Standing at the edge of death,
that's where magnanimity ends
and rising on my left elbow,
I plunged the knife in with my right hand.

I was told in the morning that he'd survived,
God saved us both,
the end of a duel's unknown in the beginning.
One of the two must survive.

Were there no eye witnesses or spectators?
Our knives were on all their lips,
and my name sounded loudly,
I'd have no regrets if he died.

But do you know that
'that' counts for nothing,
I both admit and regret
the kind of life whittled out
if you obediently follow the law.

All the roads lead to Rome,
but it seems not all of them go to the Law.
A puff of wind extinguishes the candle,
it's alight when the weather is nice.

You want to imprison me for so many days?
I'm asking you,

how will it harm you

if you don't count days in a prison cell,

but, instead, keep your nose to yourself?

Why are you staring at the knife?

Look at the Semiramide Gardens,

I followed the rising sun,

I'll set it like a garnet in a royal mantle.

What do you want to hear? Come on, tell me.

You're looking for guilt in me,

I'm looking for a human being in a guilty man,

we've travelled different roads with different aptitudes.

Stick to your own people whom you've crowned,

although we've the same heaven and clothes,

my dream won't coincide

with your advertising brochure.

Your questions have already gone mouldy,

I expect freshness from you in vain,

you're asking where I worked:

I rang the chapel bell.

Sometimes I was Baron of the gypsies,

sometimes I wore stolen furs,

and everywhere I used the same password,

as in heaven, I'm free from the Law of Gravity.

Although the cross has wooden wings,
and Newton's Law of Gravity pulled my reins,
Sir Isaac would be disappointed,
you can't keep me here on earth.

I haven't lived like a butterfly,
I've held the handle of a knife,
and, for joy and regret, I have
a star nurtured in my heart.

ChapterXXIX Letter to Heraclius

Hey Heraclius!

I too stuck poles in the waters of Venice,

trimmed in the still water,

I built a pole forest,

so the gondolas can slide freely

through the narrow streets,

so serenades will be sung

by the gondolier,

so the couple can open

wide their windows,

so the steamy bed

will be covered with beauty.

I stuck the poles in the waters of Venice,

as landmarks

in the water's dangerous surface

to watch out for,

and with the trimmed wooden poles

I marked the border:

- Between death and life,

- Between evil and kindness,

- Between hatred and love.

So the poet's verse

written on this border

will remain as a road sign

at the crossroads:

- This way to life!

- To kindness!

- To love!
- To Venice!

Chapter XXX   Without Protocol

One question, Mr Ponti,
a question unrelated to the case,
you're surrounded by colleagues,
why does nobody defend you?

Your Honour, if you allow me,
I'll explain as best I can,
why no one shows any passion,
why no one cranes their necks at the windows.

Why don't they stand on tiptoes,
to catch a glance of the Lady Justice's chamber?
The poet just sits happily at home,
willingly helping himself to sherbet.

When a man is being sacrificed,
a large rock drops from their decrepit shoulders,
they measure the distance to eternity,
everyone separately,
or else collectively.

That's how people in the provinces get high,
as if puffing on a powerful joint
and they believe no one can sing as well,
as at our place, here in our country.

Even incest can lead to reproduction
and has its explanation,
they can't find their equals,
party animals take over the space,
perform the role of poet.

The stage of the provincial theatre,
is seen as the promised land,
there's an abundance of would-be poets,
each knows the following perfectly well:

So that people feel the stroke of your pen,
so you don't stay far away from them,
your own verse should have the effect of an orgasm,
your body and voice should quiver and tremble.

If you should faint whilst reading,
they'll think you're really talented,
even though it's only drizzling, not raining,
the stalls are getting wet with the heavy downpour.

You must make them think that a demon
has caught you in its claws,
when you scrunch your eyes up above,
you'll flirt with the role of victim.

Usual greetings should confuse you,
so that no one thinks you're mortal,
or you should turn in other direction,
since you are particularly musical.

So as not to destroy the cycle of the play,
you'll smell triple-distilled vodka,
and be surprised by everyone around,
as if you've just come down from heaven.

Your Honour, I couldn't appear at this meeting,
like a person of the brand you described.
I've preferred a destiny as one christened alone
 at one baptismal font, rather than by group baptism.

That Juggler in the clown's costume
fences the ball with his nose
and sparkling eye,
if you offer him a green field,
he'll stand in the centre like a topiaried tree.

Do you remember when the talent erupted,
 the poison in the stalls, together with applause?
 The incomparable skill of Kipiani
 and the critical spectators?

Perhaps this is
Alpha and Omega,
hurray to the loyal clowns of the circus!
Those people who live in the country can't bear poets
so they open their arms to the clowns.

Their words will somersault out of their mouths,
as they keep night vigils of the glass of wine,
they learn their party pieces by heart,
for friendship and for feasting.

Useless passionate debates are raving,
the role of poet belongs to Narcissus,
the periphery finds it difficult to deal with poets,
a crystal criticises simplicity.

Your Honour, I have never had such a big escort,
I've never run anywhere ever,
I've never played the role of an eccentric,
I have never shone with a glassy facade.

I modestly admired the silk shawl of the lover,
I did not fold the lines with flirtatious intentions,
the celebration was painful to me, as I wrote,
at the edge of holding back tears.

Chapter XXXI Hurray, we're alive!

They seem to be combing the hair of your tidy daughter,
the mirror showed the loose ribbon in her hair.
Snow began to fall in the prison yard
at the very moment the letter fell from Noah's Ark.

Chapter XXXII Azdak's Recollections

Why has the blood of our sons dried up,

our women's tears dried up? I am asking the reason.

Why?

This question repeats down the ages,

like a model on a catwalk in different dresses.

All accusations are levelled at a parent.

We carry out attacks like warriors,

we took towns and villages at no great cost,

and we've taken on the role of moral arbiter.

When you increasingly remonstrate with your father:

Why did he survive?

Why wasn't he killed?

When you present him with such bold accusations,

you're showing an unresolved father complex.

Members of the congregation cross themselves in minibuses

when they catch a glance of the dome of the Holy Trinity

and by cursing our own fathers,

we are move away from being fathers to our children.

This is the lot of our epoch,

the epochal feeling of the new,

so when the prodigal son returns,

he'll find the house waiting empty.

Chapter XXXIII Letter to Odysseus

Hey, Odysseus,

it's only your own household

who are aware of your presence or absence.

Turn back this doomed

white boat!

Rembrandt, The Return of the Prodigal Son (fragment)

Chapter XXXIV The Return

Out of many roads, only the one marked N
has carnations dropped from the funeral cortege.
The ancient apartment contains only a Steinway
in the room from which the old Maestro was carried out.

The ray of sunshine faded on the medal,
arguments in the yard also ceased for a minute,
the orphaned piano,
the neighbours bowing their heads.

This once mighty household
remembers the graciousness of the Ponti family,
there are two rooms in the building
that were left to the old master's descendants.

The Pontis had the keys of the house,
when they were presented with the list of tenants.
He who introduced musical notation to Giacomo
is the one whom the procession bore away today.

This day coincided with his escape too,
Giacomo Ponti ran away from his armed escort,
the old fir trees assisted him,
protecting him from the whip against the shoulder.

He is being hunted for,
in the fields,
in the wind,
just like the wind in the field,
by the orderly march of the police,
in red and yellow
describing a black circle with a compass.

He will pray in his father's house,
and what a fine house this is,
where the fragrance of aged walls
always gives a sensation of the new.

It lives in you, everywhere and always,
far from the motherland with her pressing desires.
The taste of granny's cooking
gives a momentary shiver.

The damp smell of the old walls
you inhale as native air,
a constant tour through the archives of memory.
It comes and goes.
It comes and goes.

Sometimes the blue morning will revive,
sometimes the warm evening will revive,
dawn is breaking, the second part of your destiny is coming,
mysterious and in the moment.

The duty police
were called by my neighbour's telephone.
I can see him,
he's at home,
there's a crack in the party wall.

He plays the melody of his first rendezvous,
he plays his childhood memories of the Maestro.
He's so attached to the instrument,
it won't be difficult to find Giacomo.

He plays the universe, treacherous and sly,
he plays the wind and the bellying sails,
he plays the shirt opened by rain,
using the embankments for shelter.

***

You have the right to remain silent,
you're charged with making an escape,
you're charged with all charges without exception,
plus you're charged with attempting to cover your traces.

Where were you looking for me?
Have all traces of me disappeared?
I took delight at being in the bosom of my father's house.
Can't you see the sign on the doorway?
Giacomo Ponti lived here.

No. 14, Kazbegi Street

P.S.

I will pray in my father's house,
and what a fine house this is,
where the fragrance of aged walls
always gives a sensation of the new.

Chapter XXXV Informer Neighbour

He relied on the Word once again,

he uttered this word at the end, I swear,

'heaven',

and it sounded like,

'land ahoy'

called from the lost ship!

Chapter XXXVI Dialogue in Heaven

I can't feel signs of life nor of the grave.
Who am I, and where am I, Master?
I can see traces only of the two of us,
the blue horizon and sandy coast.

You were calling me and I followed you,
trusting in you, I was brave enough to face the phantom,
but then the trace of you would disappear.
Why did you leave me alone, my God?

From here the collapsed riverbank looks pale,
the sun and the sand are hot,
there, where there's one set of footprints,
you were tired and I was carrying you in my arms.

Chapter XXXVII Verdict

How sincere I was at the beginning of this poem,
when I listened to the stories of Christ,
and, now, I can't keep my soul in the body,
I can't keep my body on the water.

Epilogue

I am Vereli by profession, I do it as though it were a job.

From childhood I breathed it in, one being, of three beings in one,

smiles mixed with tears that appear damp on the paper,

because what is a vast country

lasts only for a second in this world.

Notes:

The title, Giocomo Ponti, alludes to 'Giacomo Joyce', a posthumously-published work by James Joyce, written in 1914, Giacomo being the Italian form of James. Ponti in Georgian means 'nonsense'.

p.38   Monica Bellucci is an Italian actress and fashion model

pp. 41-43   This chapter alludes to two historical figures:

Prince Sulkhan-Saba Orbeliani (1658-1725), a Georgian prince, writer, monk and convert to Roman Catholicism, was persecuted and dragged by his beard into an Orthodox church.

Ilia Chavchavadze (1837–1907) a Georgian writer, lawyer and nationalist was assassinated in Tsitsamuri forest.

p. 46   Luarsab Tatkaridze is a character in a story by Ilia Chavchavadze.

pp. 50-52   Samaia Gardens opens and closes with the repetition of 'eli', the Georgian word for 'wait'. This is intended to echo the original Aramaic of Christ's Word of Abandonment, 'Eli eli lama sabachthani – My God, my God, why have you forsaken me?' Samaia Gardens are in Tbilisi.

p. 66   Kipiani is a famous footballer with Dinamo Tbilisi.

p. 69   Azdak is a character in The Caucasian Chalk Circle by Bertolt Brecht.

p. 78   Vereli is an inhabitant of the Vera district of Tbilisi

Translators' acknowledgements:

A different translation of Chapter V was made at a Poetry Translation Centre workshop with Sarah Maguire (see Dato Magradze's page on www.poetrytranslation.org). We are grateful to everyone whose contribution informed our own version.

Thank you to Derek Sellen.

About the translators:

Natalia Bukia-Peters is a freelance translator, interpreter and teacher of Georgian and Russian. She studied at Tbilisi State Institute of Foreign languages before moving to New Zealand in 1992 and then to Cornwall in 1994. She is a member of the Chartered Institute of Linguists and translates from and into English.

Victoria Field is a writer and Certified Poetry Therapist. She has lived and worked in Turkey, Russia, Pakistan and Cornwall, and is now based in Canterbury. She writes poetry, fiction and drama, and has co-edited three books on therapeutic writing. She was a Hawthornden Fellow in 2012.